Crabapples

A B Sea

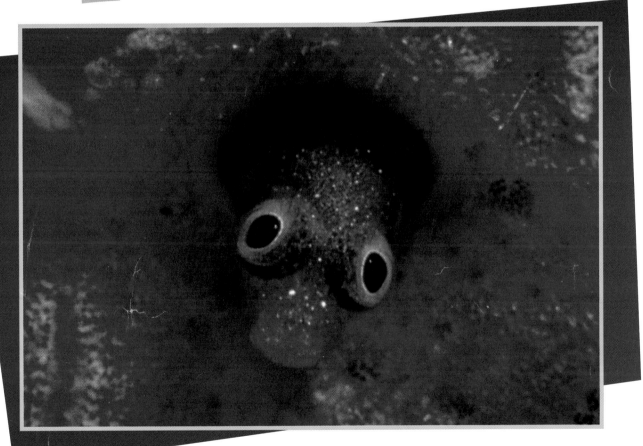

Bobbie Kalman

 Crabtree Publishing Company

www.Crabtreebooks.com

Crabapples

created by Bobbie Kalman

For Brian

Editor-in-Chief
Bobbie Kalman

Managing editor
Lynda Hale

Editors
Tammy Everts
Petrina Gentile
Niki Walker
Greg Nickles

Research
Niki Walker
Tammy Everts

Computer design
Rose Campbell

Color separations and film
Dot 'n Line Image Inc.

Illustrations
Barb Bedell: page 6
Tammy Everts: page 32
Jeannette McNaughton-Julich:
    pages 30-31

Special thanks to
Nicola Hill and Paul H. Humann

Photographs
Mike Bacon/Tom Stack & Associates: page 25
Curtis Boggs/EarthWater Stock Photography: pages 7, 11 (top),
    18 (bottom)
Bob Cranston: page 14 (top)
Chris A. Crumley/EarthWater Stock Photography: page 9 (right)
David Cubbin/EarthWater Stock Photography: page 12
Dave B. Fleetham/Tom Stack & Associates: cover
David Gilchrist: pages 24, 26
Tim Grollimund/EarthWater Stock Photography: page 18 (top)
Christopher Hartley: pages 13, 29
Kenneth J. Howard: title page, page 22 (both)
Paul H. Humann: page 15
Paul L. Janosi: pages 4, 5 (both), 10, 20, 27 (both), 28
Bobbie Kalman: page 17 (both)
Larry Lipsky/Tom Stack & Associates: page 8
Brian Parker/Tom Stack & Associates: pages 14 (bottom), 23
Charles Seaborn/Odyssey Productions: page 19
Michele C. Sistrunk/EarthWater Stock Photography: page 21
Mark Strickland/EarthWater Stock Photography: pages 9 (left),
    11 (bottom), 16

Crabtree Publishing Company

PMB 16A
350 Fifth Avenue
Suite 3308
New York
N.Y. 10118

612 Welland Avenue
St. Catharines
Ontario, Canada
L2M 5V6

73 Lime Walk
Headington
Oxford OX3 7AD
United Kingdom

Cataloging in Publication Data
Kalman, Bobbie, 1947-
    A...B...Sea

(Crabapples)
Includes index.

ISBN 0-86505-625-0 (library bound)   ISBN 0-86505-725-7 (pbk.)
A range of underwater plant and animal species, including the
lionfish, jellyfish, and coral reef, appears in this alphabet book.

1. Marine fauna - Juvenile literature. 2. English language -
Alphabet - Juvenile literature. I. Title. II. Series: Kalman,
Bobbie, 1947- . Crabapples.

QL122.2.K35 1995   j591.92 E 20   LC 95-36476
                                                 CIP

What is in this book?

is for **anemone**. An anemone on land is a flower, but a sea anemone is an animal. Sea anemones are **carnivores** that eat small fish. They use their long **tentacles** to sting their prey and scoop it into their mouth. This is a giant sea anemone.

is for **burrfish**. Burrfish do not have scales. They have tough skin and sharp spines. When a burrfish senses danger, it swallows lots of water. Soon it looks like a balloon with nails poking out of it.

is for **coral reef**. Coral reefs are made of millions of coral animals. Some are alive and some are dead. There are many kinds of coral. How many can you see in the picture?

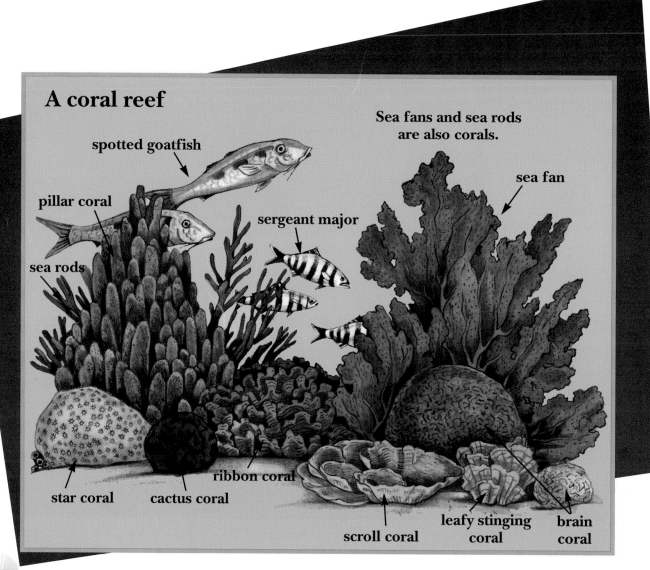

A coral reef

Sea fans and sea rods are also corals.

spotted goatfish

sea fan

pillar coral

sergeant major

sea rods

star coral

cactus coral

ribbon coral

scroll coral

leafy stinging coral

brain coral

Thousands of fish, plants, and sea creatures live in coral reefs because plenty of food can be found there. Some coral reefs are close to shore, and others are far out in the ocean.

is for **damselfish**. There are 235 kinds of damselfish! Small damselfish eat plants and tiny animals. The large ones eat crabs and shrimps. Damselfish purr and click to attract other damselfish. They also make noises to scare away enemies.

is for **eel**. An eel looks like a snake, but it is a fish. Eels have smooth skin instead of rough scales. Their teeth are sharp. Eels hunt fish and crabs at night. They hide during the day. The blue eel in the picture is a ribbon eel. The spotted one is a moray eel.

 is for **flamingo tongue**. The flamingo tongue is a type of sea snail. Most land snails have hard shells over their skin, but this snail wears its colorful skin over its shell! Flamingo tongues live on sea fans.

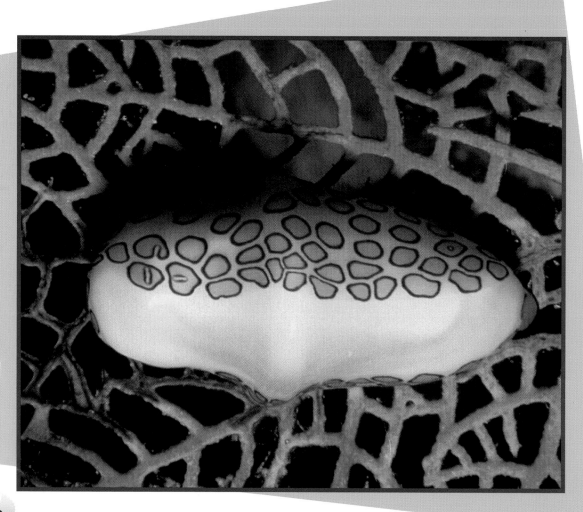

is for **goby**. Gobies are tiny fish that love to clean. They set up **cleaning stations** that bigger fish visit. Gobies eat the **parasites** that cling to the teeth, gills, and scales of larger fish. Can you see the busy goby at work?

is for **hogfish**. The colorful hogfish has a snout that looks like a hog's snout. Not only does this fish look like a hog, it acts like one, too. Just as hogs root for food on land, hogfish dig for meals on the ocean floor.

is for **isopod**. Ocean isopods are parasites. They cling to the head or gills of fish and feed off their **host**. This isopod lives on a soldierfish. Its color blends in so well that it looks as if it is part of the fish.

is for **jellyfish**. A jellyfish is not a fish at all. It is an animal that is mostly water. A jellyfish has long tentacles that hang down from its round **float**. The tentacles are covered with stingers that can kill small fish and hurt larger creatures.

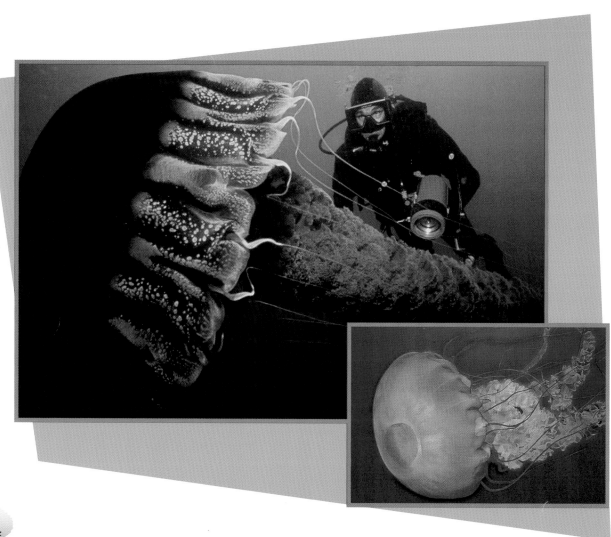

is for **king helmet shell**. The king helmet shell is a type of sea snail. This snail usually hides in its shell, but sometimes its mouth and tentacles stick out of the opening. The snail's shell grows as the snail grows.

is for **lionfish**. When the lionfish spreads its **pectoral fins**, they look like a lion's mane. The fins scare away enemies. The lionfish also uses its fins to sweep fish, shrimp, and crabs toward its wide mouth. Its **dorsal fins** have poisonous spines.

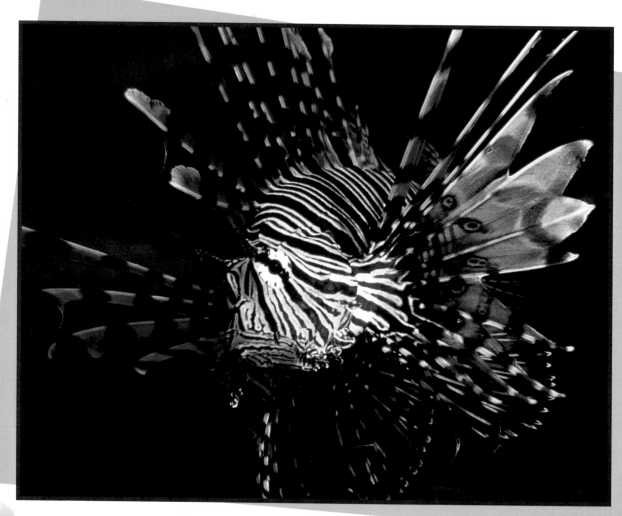

is for **mammal**. Whales, seals, sea lions, walruses, and sea otters are all mammals that live in the ocean. Dolphins are mammals, too. They are part of the whale family. All mammals need to breathe air. Dolphins breathe air through their **blowhole**.

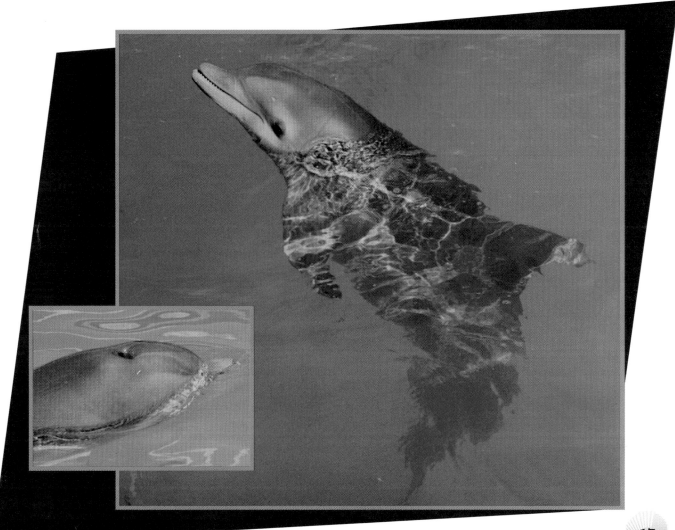

is for **nurse shark**. Sharks are fish. A nurse shark has a feeler, or **barbel**, on each side of its mouth. It uses its barbels to find food in the sand. Nurse sharks like to lie on the ocean floor. They make a sucking noise that sounds like a nursing baby.

is for **octopus**. Octopuses live in caves and holes near the bottom of the ocean. They hunt at night. They squirt dark ink into the water to hide from enemies. If an octopus loses a tentacle, it can grow a new one. Octopuses are very intelligent.

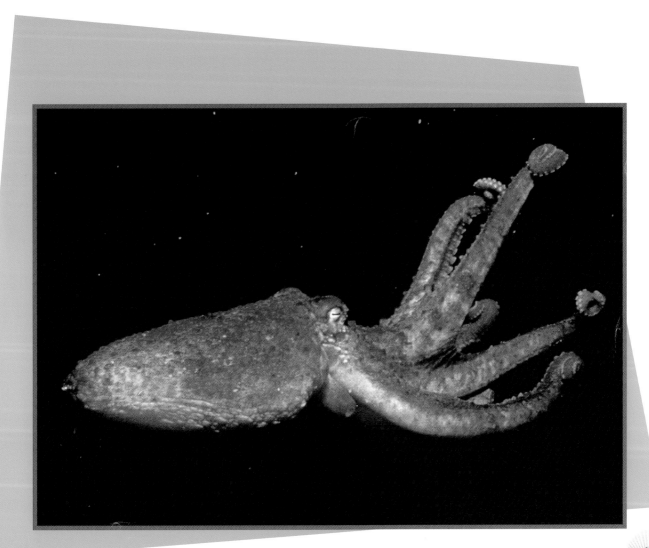

is for **parrotfish**. The parrotfish looks like a parrot. It is colorful and has a sharp beak. The parrotfish is a noisy eater. It feeds on small plants that live on coral reefs. It also bites off chunks of hard coral.

is for **queen triggerfish**. These fish are very fierce. They will attack any creature that comes too close to their home. Triggerfish have strong jaws to crack the shell of their favorite prey—giant clams.

is for **ray**. There are several kinds of rays. The swimming ray in the picture below is an eagle ray. The one in the sand is a stingray. Using their flat fins, rays seem to fly under water. A ray's mouth is on the underside of its body.

is for **seahorse**. This small fish is a weak swimmer. It stays upright and holds onto objects with its **prehensile** tail. It wraps its tail around plants to keep from being swept away by strong ocean currents.

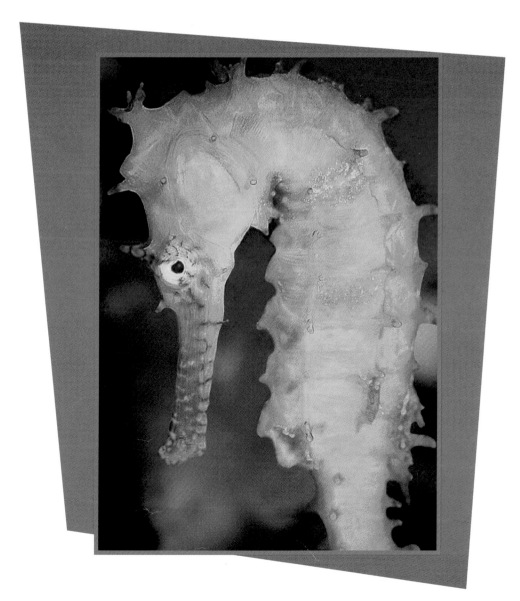

is for **trunkfish**. The trunkfish belongs to the boxfish family. From the side, it looks like a box. Instead of scales, the trunkfish is covered in bony plates that protect it from other creatures. Trunkfish also release a deadly poison for protection.

is for **urchin**. There are over 700 kinds of sea urchins. A sea urchin's sharp spines keep enemies away. The sea urchin has no eyes or brain. Its mouth is on the underside of its body. It sticks out its teeth to scrape sea plants from rocks.

is for **Venus sea fan**. Sea fans are a type of coral. Venus sea fans live in shallow, clear water near coral reefs. They have tiny branches that are woven together like a net. They catch food in these branches. Venus sea fans are yellow, gray, or purple.

 is for **worm**. Over 5000 kinds of worms live in the sea. The sea worms below are called feather duster worms because their **crown** looks just like a feather duster. If something frightens this worm, it pulls its crown into its body tube.

is for **xestospongia muta**, the scientific name for giant barrel sponge. The big opening at the top of the sponge is called the **oscula**. Giant barrel sponges are large enough to fit a diver inside!

is for yellowtail snapper. Yellowtail snappers swim above reefs and are not afraid of people. They are curious and will come very close to divers. These yellowtail snappers must wonder where the party is!

is for **zones of life**. There are living things at every level of the ocean. Sea plants and animals help keep the ocean healthy.

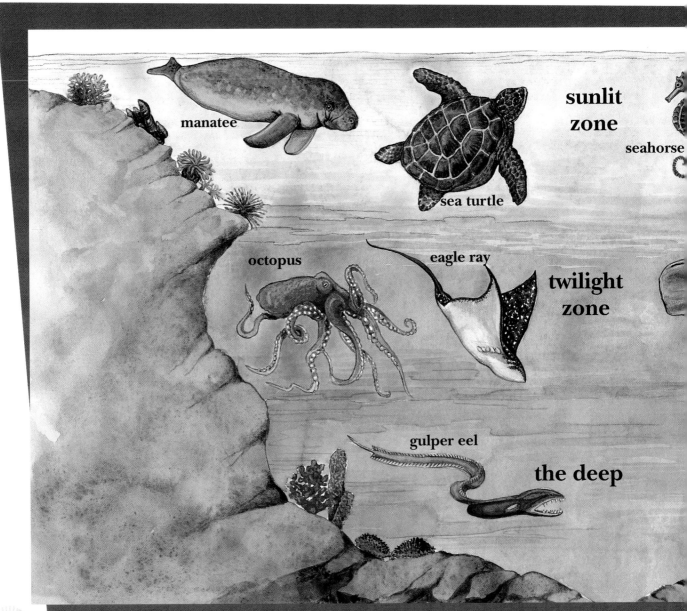

manatee

sunlit zone

seahorse

sea turtle

octopus

eagle ray

twilight zone

gulper eel

the deep

The sunlit zone, twilight zone, and the deep are three zones of ocean life. Coral reefs are part of the sunlit zone.

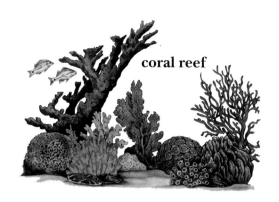

coral reef

Portuguese man-of-war

jellyfish

angelfish

butterflyfish

sperm whale

moray eel

squid

manta ray

angler fish

The **sunlit zone** gets a lot of light. Most fish, sea grasses, and seaweeds live in the sunlit zone.

The **twilight zone** is darker and colder than the sunlit zone. Sponges, corals, octopuses, rays, and squid live at this level. Some whales dive down to the twilight zone to feed.

The **deep** is very dark and cold. Sea worms, sea cucumbers, and corals live on the ocean floor. The deep is home to unusual fish such as the gulper eel and the angler fish.

Words to know

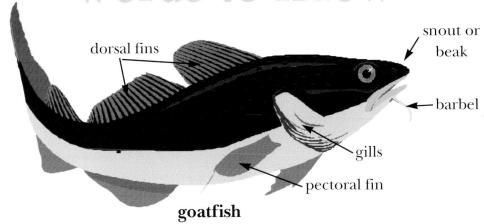

dorsal fins

snout or
beak

barbel

gills

pectoral fin

goatfish

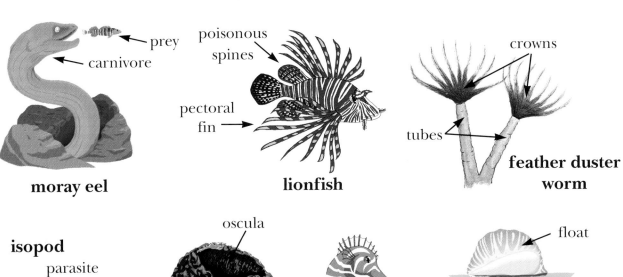

prey

carnivore

moray eel

poisonous
spines

pectoral
fin

lionfish

crowns

tubes

**feather duster
worm**

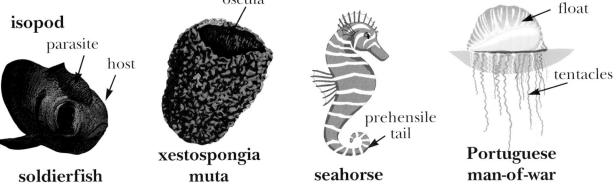

isopod

parasite

host

soldierfish

oscula

**xestospongia
muta**

prehensile
tail

seahorse

float

tentacles

**Portuguese
man-of-war**

9 0 Printed in the U.S.A.   3 2 1